Why Men Have Problems With Women

By
Joe G. Morin

Copyright © 2013
ISBN-13: 978 0615863436
Published 2013

For more information contact:
Joe G. Morin
JoeGMorin@gmail.com

Lyrics and Books From the Heart Publishing Company, Inc.
Knoxville, Tennessee

This book is dedicated to men and written from a man's point of view. Each poem deals with the trials, tribulations, and joys of being a man. Only a man can understand the problems they have with women. However, each man also understands the uniqueness and pride of being a man.

Table of Contents

Why Men Have Problems With Women

The problems with women are that they're always right
A man can never tell them they're wrong without a fight
A woman's feelings are too easily hurt
Therefore a man must always be on alert

A woman makes too much out of little things
A man doesn't worry about what tomorrow brings
A woman has many needs to fulfill
A man doesn't have the time or the will

A woman wants to be heard and talk things out
A man has heard it all before and wants to shout
A woman is like an elephant and never forgets
A man doesn't want to be reminded of his regrets

Men like to shout and yell and wonder why
Women take that as if it gives them a reason to cry
Men think women are too touchy and bitch too much
Women think men are like the wild bunch

A woman needs to know men act like men
A woman thinks they act like children
A man knows that he needs a woman
A woman makes him feel like a man

Women Get What They Want

Many women think men are dumb
Men just act stupid to have fun
Women communicate differently
Men are used to being talked to directly

Men think about love and relationships too
Women think men know nothing about those two
Love has two meanings for men
That's the way it's always been

They think men have just one thing on their mind
They know that men can't have only a good time
Men don't always think about love making
They think just as much about drinking

Men play dumb when they make a mistake
Especially when their idea was half-baked
They fear that a woman may not understand
That they sometimes need a helping hand

Men want to think they are romantic and loving
They don't realize women are more cunning
Women take advantage of men's one track mind
That's why women get what they want every time

I've Got a Question

A man never wants to hear "I've got a question"
What will follow can only cause him indigestion
He knows his answer will never satisfy
Making him wish that he could run and hide

He can only hope for a short interruption
Maybe she will forget her assumption
But he knows that she will ask it again
And he knows how badly this will end

When he gives his answer to her question
He braces himself for an inquisition
Because there will be further questions
And she don't care about his opinions

Perhaps the moral to this story is key
To whatever the question may be
Men know their answer will always fail
They need to say I'm not feeling well

We Need to Talk

"We need to talk" will make a man's heart stop
They strike terror and make his head drop
Coming from a woman can only mean
He will be wishing this day was only a bad dream

The first thing on his mind
What did I do this time
He thinks about what he must have done
But knows only the worst is going to come

His mind races, and he starts to sweat
His thoughts are in overdrive and yet
He knows that this is not going to be pretty
He hopes that this will blow over in a hurry

Her next words may seal his fate
He's thinking of excuses before it's too late
If only he'd been more attentive
He wouldn't have to be so inventive

As she starts to speak
He begins to get weak
The first rule is clear
Always say the words "Yes, dear "

Never Say You Just Forgot

Man must remember everything
Because he will always catch the blame
If he forgets the littlest thing
A woman will drive him insane

No matter how many things are on his mind
He needs to take notes all the time
He should know better and put
Important dates in his address book

She may be the prettiest girl in the world
But she will make your hair curl
If you forget that important date
You know what will be your fate

She will give you the silent treatment
Be very careful before you make a statement
Never say these words if you are caught
It's better to plead insanity then say "you forgot"

You Can Never Please Them

A honey do list she may make
Sometimes isn't too hard to take
But remember that this list can be
The thing that can drive you up a tree

You may try to do everything right
You may try to stay out of sight
You may feel that you did better
But they are birds of a different feather

You may think that you went the extra miles
You think that they will be all smiles
When the jobs are done and complete
You know you won't take any more heat

You have done all the chores you had
You know they will be glad
But if you do one thing wrong
You will hear about it all week long

Men Show Love Differently

Women think men have no mind
That men think about sex all the time
It may be true about some men
Men show love differently than women

Women think men always want some
That they behave like a real bum
Women think men cheat and steal
Just to get a little feel

Women want their men's desire hot
So that their love will never stop
Women always want to be adored
And not hear a man just say he scored

Women should know what a wise woman said
Men don't talk about the feelings in their head
They show love differently than women
That's why sex may be something more to men

First Kiss

It came on a summer's night
In the last of a day's light
In a moment of fire
In a moment of desire

The color of her hair
Was brown and light as air
Her laughter and smile so sassy
We were so young and happy

The summer night felt magical
With a hint of something mystical
As we held hands in the twilight
With the stars coming out so bright

In the soft light our first kiss
It was pure bliss
Our lips touched that night
So tenderly and so tight

We made magic that night
Until dawn's early light
Love was in the air
We did not have a care

Now as I look at the twilight sky
I have a warm tear in my eye
Filled with memories of that night
So tender and so right

Women Will Make Men Crazy

Men may pride themselves as smart
They may even dress and look the part
Men may be successful or lazy
But women will make men crazy

You see, men don't understand
What a woman can do to a man
A man doesn't have a clue
What a lovely woman can do

Men think they are the hunter
But to women they are just butter
Women know how to make men melt
Because men think below the belt

Men think they are in control
But before they can strike the first blow
A woman will turn the table
And put him in the stable

Women are something that men need
But women know how to make men bleed
Women scheme and make plans also
Men want to make it up as they go

So men one thing before you leave
Women have something up their sleeve
You better not think you know it all
Women know how to drive you up a wall

What Women Won't Tell You to Say

Women don't tell you everything
It's like the words to a song men can't sing
They feel that men can always find
A way to say what's on their mind

Men don't always "get it" women say
But men should know it anyway
Men may think they know what to do
But men don't have a clue

Men don't think about what they'd said
Women don't understand what's in their head
Men expect women to tell them the words
But the words escape them like flying birds

It's hard for men to say the words at first
That women expect for better or worst
Men don't always express things in word
Leaving women to wonder if they ever heard

Women want to hear from her man
To say the words as best as he can
To them it's as simple as the clouds above
All he has to say is that "It's you I love"

All Women Do Is Nag

Every man dreads this when it comes
It makes men feel they're all bums
Women just want to make a point
This makes men wish they were in a beer joint

All men have at least one fault
Some men play too much golf
Some men forget to do their chores
Some men won't mop the floors

Men may lack in one or more thing
But he doesn't want to take the blame
If he wants to have any fun at all
He'll just smile and take the fall

Women just don't talk about it once
They seem to want to talk about it a bunch
It seems to him he will hear about it for days
Please, please, I want some quiet he prays

So when she starts to nag
He thinks about packing his bag
No one wants to be told they are a fool
To men that is something that seems cruel

Men hate to hear women nag
So women put it in a bag
Men will love you for this, honey
They will gladly give you their money

Men's Secret

Men will look at women all day long
Women to them are like a beautiful song
Each curve has its own power
Like the blossom of a wild flower

They can't wait to see her smile
This to see, they would walk a mile
To see a smile on her face
Is like a dress with delicate lace

Men try to look into a woman's eyes
They know that eyes don't tell lies
They hope that her eyes will shine
To let them know what's on her mind

Women are a mystery to men
But they can't do without them
Men want to treat them right
But men are not always that bright

So mothers please do women a favor
Teach your sons about women's behavior
Men need to know this to be a woman's man
Men's secret is that men just don't understand

A Woman Can Make a Man

Men may look like they are on top
They don't always know what they've got
A good woman can make her man
This a man must understand

A woman holds power over her man
Break him or make him she can
Women know men's weakness
But smart women know their business

They want their man to be a success
They don't want their man to be a mess
Men sometimes get lost and must find their way
Women can help them reminding them each day

Women need to help keep men on track
She's the one who has got his back
Men need to know this all the time
Women who do this will do just fine

Today, women are smart and have careers
Women have their own goals and cares
So women when you think your job's done
Remember that making a man can be fun

A Night Out With the Boys

Every man knows that he must get away
He has got to have time to play
Women need to know how important this is
For him to relieve that stress of his

He needs sometimes to act like one of the boys
He's got to play with his big toys
Whether or not it's his 4 wheel drive truck
Or playing poker with the boys for a buck

Men are like horses you see
They sometimes got to run free
They need to act like they have no cares
Like a little boy sliding down the stairs

They may drink a little too much
But don't raise too much of a fuss
Being a man has expectations
And life is full of frustrations

Being with the boys is not so bad
Don't let it make you women mad
It lets them release some steam
Like a dam full of water in a stream

So girls don't fret too much
He'll still love you a bunch
Because after time with the boys
You will look much lovelier than his toys   17

Men's Love

A man has many types of love
Like the different clouds above
Some are big and soft and fine
Others are light and kind

To his woman a man will give
All his love and heart that is his
She brings him joy and happiness
And makes his life make sense

To his children a man will give
All his love and heart that is his
He will always wish that he had been
Like his father and played more with them

To his dog a man will give
All his love and heart that is his
He will wonder where time has went
Because she was such a loving pet

To his parents a man will give
All his love and heart that is his
He will remember when he was a boy
And when they gave him his first big toy

To his life a man will give
All his love and heart that is his
He will know how precious it was
When he looks down from above

Why I Am Glad to Go

It was a warm April of that year
We didn't seem to have a care
We were so much in love
As we watched the clouds above

We met long before that day
We had both went to a play
I noticed her as she walked by
And at once she caught my eye

I couldn't help myself but stare
Should I talk to her or do I dare
I walked over to her hoping to see
If she would talk to me

It was that day, I fell in love
I can't forget how wonderful it was
The warm nights of quiet passion
The mornings of soft reflection

Every April we went on a picnic
The mountains were turning green and yet
We knew that we had more years to spend
Every day in love and raising our children

I remember the sound of the rain
When the angels came
She had left the earth a year or so
That's why I am glad to go

A Boy's First Date

I remember my first date
I was almost late
I was just a young lad
It wasn't all that bad

It took all my nerve to ask her
But to my surprise she said sure
I didn't know how to reply
I shyly said see you tomorrow, bye

It was during summer break
I cleaned the car that I would take
My dad and mom just smiled at me
They couldn't just let me be

I tried to look so cool
I didn't want to be a fool
When it was time to go, you see
I felt as nervous as could be

I drove to her house scared to death
Full of anxiety, and out of breath
I didn't know how to talk to a girl
They came from a different world

I walked to her door with great care
I hoped her parents would not be there
But her father met me at the door
I knew I was in trouble for sure

He looked at me up and down
I thought I must look like a clown
But he smiled at me because he knew
That it was probably my first date too

Women Don't Always Get Along

Most men know that there should be a song
That says women don't usually get along
Men used to think women were always tight
But soon they learn women must love to fight

Let one woman think she got disrespected
She will give back more than anyone expected
Women just don't forgive and forget
Once they start, you haven't seen anything yet

Women should be careful what they say
They seem to want the other one to pay
They will plot and try to seek revenge
Men don't know when it will ever end

Men should know better than get involved
They will never get the matter resolved
They need to remember the cardinal rule
A man that gets involved is a fool

So women, please talk things out
You have other things to worry about
If women would take this energy and plot
Women would always remain on top

Men Are Not the Only Hunters

Men think they are the only ones that hunt
But women know what men want
Women watch and study their prey
But men are naïve, they don't see it that way

A man may think he is very smart
He will look and act the part
He will look at the women in a certain way
But women know who's the prey

Women know they are safe in packs
They know all the facts
Men try to look and conceal what they want
But women know when men are on the hunt

Men are silly, but they are not to blame
Women are taught how to play this game
Men think too much with their lower brain
That's why women will win just the same

Women know how to lure in their prey
They know how to keep men at bay
Women are patient and wait for the best time
To sneak up and get them from behind

So men should know this about women
The female is the best hunter in the end
That's why at home the male lion will stay
Because the female lion always gets her prey

Girls Forget That Boys Become Men

Girls forget that boys become men
Sometimes girls have little use for them
Girls think boys are silly and dumb
But men are what boys become

Girls think boys are only gross
That boys will only boast
Boys think girls are no fun
Until a certain age girls become

Girls are ahead of boys
Girls want more than just toys
That's when it all will begin
When boys start looking like men

Girls will look at boys differently
When boys start looking at girls closely
Girls will start to flirt then
When boys start becoming men

Boys need to remember about girls
That they sometimes want more than pearls
It's when boys know what they will get when
Girls don't forget boys become men

Little White Lies

Often it's the little white lies men tell
That keeps men's lives from going to hell
Women often ask a loaded question
That men wish they wouldn't mention

If she asks you about her new dress
You can't tell her it looks like a mess
If she asks you does this make me look fat
You don't dare tell her that's a fact

If she asks you about her brother
You can't tell her that he's a loser
If she asks you about her mother
You can't tell her she's a monster

If she asks does this color look good on me
You can't say that it makes her look like a tree
If she asks you about her best friend
Don't say you knew her way back when

A white lie sometimes comes in handy
It will coat the truth with a little candy
The truth can sometimes be hard to take
So a white lie men will make

Women, please remember just don't ask
If his answer may be your man's last
Some questions you may never get the truth
If the answer may send you thru the roof

I'm Not the Sharpest Knife in the Drawer

Some men think they are very smart
But to tell you the truth they aren't
Some men think they can get away with it
But the truth is not even a little bit

Some men think women are dumb
But they are just a bunch of horse dung
Some men think women are easy
But they are just thinking with their Willy

Some men think they know it all
But they usually are in for a fall
Some men think women are only for show
But they usually have to eat crow

Some men think women need their support
But women just use them for sport
Some men think the world revolves around them
But women know it's not all about him

Men should treat women with respect
Some men don't know that yet
I might not be a sharpest knife in the drawer
But I know women want more

There Are Two Ways to Fix Things

Men never let a woman help you fix anything
They will only drive you insane
You know how to fix it with care
But fixing things with women can be a bear

You may think they will be a great help
But you will only make a fool of yourself
Men think they can fix it very quickly
But with a woman that can go quite differently

Men don't want women to ever know
That they don't know where a part should go
Men want to show their stuff
Women know how to call their bluff

If you should ever have women help you
Don't let them make you lose your cool
If you do something wrong, and they are right
Just don't say a thing until they are out of sight

Please remember something that is true
If your lover is helping you
Just remember all the good things they've done
And later you may have much more fun

Of Men Treating Them Like a Queen

Men may want to become a king
But women want to feel like a queen
Men may want to be like the pirates at sea
But women want to feel like a queen bee

A man may want to give his woman riches
Especially if she gives him hugs and kisses
A man has his dreams of great fame
A woman wants the very same thing

A man may want to be in control
But a woman knows that isn't so
A man may think he's a big deal
But his fate, a woman can seal

A woman wants the fine things in life
She wants to feel the softness of the night
She wants what she thinks she's worth
She wants love and not hurt

Men need to treat their women well
Like a queen in a storybook tale
Women want to have their dream
Of men treating them like a queen

She Can Steal Your Heart Too

So son, let me tell you a story
That will teach you not to be sorry
Young men are not always smart
If the wrong woman steals their heart

When you are young and like many men
You will know nothing about certain women
Many women can be a sight to behold
But they can also be very cold

A beautiful woman can cast a spell
Before a young man can tell
She has taken his heart
And torn his world apart

Young men, you need to open your eyes
A woman can be the devil that lies
She can take your money and pride
And to a place that has a dark side

There are women that are fine
But be careful of who you find
Don't let the wrong woman get to you
Because she can steal your heart too

Women's Changing Minds

Women will change their mind
They seem to do this all the time
This will drive men insane
And it's not men who's to blame

Men are as stubborn as a mule
And never want to change as a rule
Women's minds change like the wind
That's why men can't seem to win

Men are asked what they want to do
If they answer they're a fool
With women, men may discuss things
Only to find changes the next day brings

Women change their minds and don't care
That's why there are so many styles of hair
Women try to choose what to wear ahead
But change their mind after a night in bed

Men need to think about this
Or their life will be a mess
A woman will change her mind
As sure as the sun will shine

Men, Never Give Your Opinion

Men, your opinion will never do
And you will regret it too
If a woman asks for your opinion
Just pretend that you can't hear them

To give an opinion about what a woman's said
Caused many a man to be filled with dread
Your opinion better be what she wants to hear
Or you will pay for it all year

Men should know what to say if asked
They should always think real fast
Their life may depend on what they say
If they want to live in peace for another day

If she asks you about her mother
Just start talking about your brother
You must live with both of them
So say, "It's just a misunderstandin"

So men know that this is true
Your opinion can make your life blue
So when she asks you for your opinion
Please notify your next of kin

Men Love Their Children Too

Men don't get the credit they're due
They love their children too
Men don't always show it on the outside
They think their soft side they must hide

Women and children are a loving sight
But men aren't seen in the same light
Men smile and have a big grin
When they have time with their children

A child can sense their father's love
It's a gift from the one above
A child wants their father to care
And wants to know he will be there

Mothers give their children many things
It's other things that their father brings
Mothers nurture their children with care
Fathers give children all the love they can spare

Next time you see children with their family
Make sure you take time to see
And you will realize that it is true
Men love their children too

Without You All I Can Do Is Cry

Why did you leave our beautiful home?
I don't want to live here all alone
I keep wondering what and why
Without you all I can do is cry

We were so much in love
Joined like the sky and clouds above
Two people with so much life ahead
Now I feel just sorrow and dread

The years have come and gone
But my love for you is still strong
My heart is breaking more each day
Filled with my memories of yesterday

I see your lovely face smiling at me
When you said our love will always be
But you must have thought there was no hope
To leave me with only a short note

It says that our life will never be the same
As when long ago I took your name
Things happen that we can't change
And there's just no one to blame

I cherish the days I had with you
Please forgive me, I hope you do
I stared at the note wondering why
Knowing without you all I can do is cry

A Man Needs His Dog and So Do You

No matter what his dog has done
A man needs his dog for some fun
So what if the old hound buried his bone
In the flowers you had just sown

Even if the old hound had a flea
He doesn't carry any disease
His dog may have come from the pound
But to him, there's no better to be found

The old hound may bark all night long
To him that's a melody from a lovely song
The old hound may just sit and lay around
But with your man, he jumps up and down

Your man loves that old dog so much
It's hard to not be jealous of the mutt
You think he treats his dog better than you
And you don't know what to do

The answer to this problem is not new
You need to keep the old hound with you
Your man will never stray or go anywhere
Missing you two is more than he could bear

Does His Work Mean More Than You

You wonder if it's really true
That his work means more than you
He says he needs to work for the pay
But does he have to work every day

You know he works for the family
But you're tired and feel up a tree
Of him working, not being around
Making you feel so sad and down

Money is also very important to you
But doesn't keep you from feeling blue
So every day without him near
Seems to last a whole full year

You try telling him you're not happy
And your children needs their daddy
But he says, "What's he to do?"
They need that money too

So please understand he's trying
He doesn't want you crying
You mean more than work, it's true
But it's something he feels he must do

Women Make You Wait

Men don't be in a hurry
Women will make your sorry
If you try to speed them up
You are pressing your luck

Women will make you wait
Especially on your first date
They want you to know
That they are in control

Men should know it takes time
For women to make up their mind
On their make-up or what to wear
Even on how to fix their hair

Men, she wants to hear that sound
When you see her come around
Of you holding your breath
And looking like you've seen the best

So men wait you will
Don't let it make you ill
Waiting is one thing you do
But waiting can be worth it too

Always Bet on the Mare

People are partial to a male horse
In a race they run a good course
A black stallion is something to behold
Because of his lines and spirit so bold

But one betting man I once knew
Said that's not always true
A mare you will see
Can make a fool out of you and me

Once he was a young buck
Losing and down on his luck
Until he met an old man
So old that he could hardly stand

He walked slowly up to him
As if he was one of his kin
That was how it began
And it made him a changed man

It was at the big races in May
The races wasn't going his way
The old man told him don't worry
And do not be in such a hurry

He said in the big race today
You will hit the big pay
But you must take care
To bet on the brown mare

He stared at the old man
As he looked down from the stand
That didn't sound so grand
The favorite was the black stallion

So he took his advice, and she won
Winning the race by a length and some
He said remember a mare that's so fine
Will always mess up a stallion's mind   **36**

Shopping Is In Their Genes

Just like a pair of fashion jeans
Shopping is in their genes
Ask a woman what she likes to do
Shopping she will reply back to you

It's the nature of their sex
Shopping for a price that's less
Money may come, and money may go
But shopping is their highest goal

They will shop until they drop
Even then they don't want to stop
Their chromosomes are arranged that way
But it's their significant other that has to pay

Their closets may be filled to capacity
But don't mind that it's only Tuesday
Christmas shopping to them is great
It gives them a reason to shop late

So men if you want to survive
And you want your love to thrive
Give them the time to shop
And their love won't stop

Women you know he's a honey
When he gives you his money
So shop away and come home
And give him more than cologne

She May Be a Witch But She's Mine

Many men have women that are fine
Mine's a witch but she's all mine
Some women are real kind
But mine's a witch all the time

Many women dress up to look fine
My woman dresses up for a good time
Many men want their women to be happy
My woman would think that's too sappy

Many women go to parties and dance
My woman would put their men in a trance
She can dance and move in a certain way
That would make dead men want to play

Many women think they are cute
My woman doesn't give a hoot
My woman is dark and very exotic
And maybe a little psychotic

Many women think they can make love for sure
My woman makes me shout for an encore
Many men want their women to be rich
I don't care because mine is a real witch

Why Don't You Love Me Like Before

Lying in bed across from you
I'm wondering what to do
You just go to bed and sleep
All I can do is try not to weep

I want to kiss your lips
And touch your lovely hips
Your skin is so soft and fair
But you say don't go there

Is this what happens to many
Their women don't want any
Do women just use their sex
To get a man and that's it

Many things go thru your mind
You remember a different time
When as lovers things were different
That making love was very passionate

Now I dread going to bed
I feel that I'm already dead
Without your love, what's life to me
It's like drowning in a dark sea

I'm not mad at you but life
But it cuts me like a knife
I still love you so
But I feel so low

Tomorrow will probably be the same
I will have nothing but the pain
I will just lie in bed wanting more
Why don't you love me like before   39

Women Don't Know Men

Women think they know men
They really don't about them
Women think they are so smart
But many times they aren't

Women think men are so dumb
They think all men want is some
Women think men are simple
And can be mashed like a pimple

Women think men need them so much
For their love and their touch
Women think men are so primitive
And they are so more inventive

What women don't know about men
Is how to keep men happy with them
They think that men don't want anything
That his feelings don't mean a thing

Women think their men are a wreck
But forget their man needs his self-respect
So women think before you say or do
If your man means anything to you

They Will Always Love Her

There's a special place for that girl
She was the prettiest one in the world
Men always remember her with a smile
They think about her once in awhile

It may have been because they were young
And innocent in the school days of fun
The girls with their long silky hair
Their eyes sparking without a care

They remember how it was then
They were awkward and not men
They didn't even know how to talk
To the pretty girl down the block

When they saw her in a different light
Their heart would race at her sight
They couldn't wait to ask her for a date
Before they knew it, it was too late

She became their first love song
Their hearts stolen before long
Their thoughts of love and more
Like the waves beating on the shore

She was young with the world at her feet
She had other plans and promises to keep
Even years later memories of her occur
They still know they will always love her

Why Nice Guys Finish Last

As the years have passed by
I'm still mad and know it's a lie
That girls are made of sugar and spice
And girls always want you to be nice

We were told that good was key
To success and making money
But it seems it's just not right
When they get everything in sight

When you see girls look and stare
Not for you, they don't care
But for the bad boys in the hall
Bad boys seem to get them all

For the boys that didn't get the grades
They had no trouble getting laid
Your reputation was good and kind
But girls wouldn't give you any time

Women want the excitement and more
They think good boys will be a bore
It may be with you they'd settle down
But now you feel like a clown

If you want women, success, and fame
Being good may be too lame
It's bad boys that gives them a blast
That's why nice guys finish last

Women Are Liars

Men don't have a chance
Women want more than romance
They say money doesn't get men anywhere
But they're liars, money makes them care

We have all seen the story before
Women like their fancy cars and more
It seems that rich men can be jerks
But money has its perks

Women are like bees looking for honey
And they like looking at the money
Women may read a romance book
But a poor man won't get a second look

Many poor boys learn it fast and quick
If you want that beautiful chick
Money is something you better get fast
Because without money you'll come in last

So when women say they don't care
Remember that life's a bear
Don't believe everything they say
They're liars about money anyway

Since the Days of Adam and Eve

Throughout history, there's always been
Differences between women and men
Since the story of Adam and Eve
A woman has always been hard to believe

Men and women have had problems for years
Men use force, women use tears
Men don't seem to understand a woman's mind
Men use money, women use their behind

Maybe it's just a cultural thing
Men want sex, women want a ring
Maybe it's just what we do
Men like red, women like blue

Whatever the problems may be
Whatever the differences we see
Sometimes men will need women
Sometimes women will need men

There are differences between women and men
That's the way it's always been
If a man and woman had not gotten along
You wouldn't be around to hear this song

About the Author

Joe Morin has worked with rural, urban, and people from all over the world through his work in Adult Education. This gives him insight into the various cultures in the world. However, it is his Southern roots that brings a common touch to his writings.

www.ingramcontent.com/pod-product-compliance
Lightning Source LLC
Chambersburg PA
CBHW060632030426
42337CB00018B/3330